# RUNES

ANCIENT WISDOM FOR THE NEW AGE

# RUNES

## THE SECRETS OF THE STONES

Anders Andersson

IMM lifestyle books
Read. Learn. Do What You Love.

Text, illustrations, and photographs by IMM Lifestyle Books, an imprint of Fox Chapel Publishing, 903 Square Street, Mount Joy, PA 17552. *www.foxchapelpublishing.com*

First published in 1997 by New Holland (Publishers) Ltd



Designed and edited by
Complete Editions
40 Castelnau
London SW13 9RU

Editorial Direction: Yvonne McFarlane
Editor: Michèle Brown
Designer: Peter Ward

ISBN 978-1-5048-0161-4

Printed in China
First Printing

FSC
www.fsc.org
MIX
Paper | Supporting responsible forestry
FSC® C147414



This is a gift book. It is not inteded to encourage diagnosis and treatment of illnesses, disease or other general problems by the layman. Any application of the recommendations set out in the following pages is at the reader's discretion and sole risk.

# CONTENTS

Across the Millenia 7
The Runes 10
Frey's Eight 13
Hagall's Eight 21
Tyr's Eight 31
Make Your Own Runes 40
How to Cast The Runes 42
The Three Norns 44
A Simple Cross Reading 46
The Celtic Cross 48
Runescripts 50
Runic Relationships 52
Gardening Runes 57
Gems and The Runes 61
ACKNOWLEDGEMENTS 64

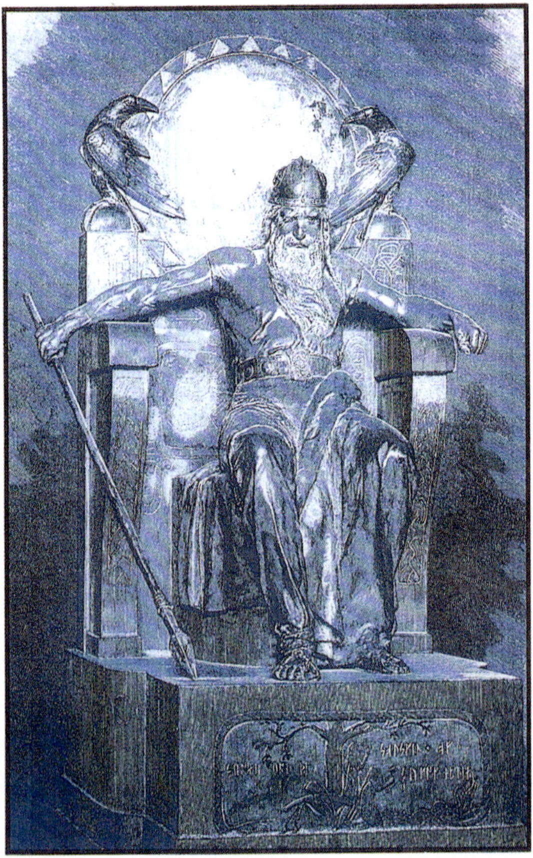

# ACROSS THE MILLENIA

Odin, the most tragic and noble of the Norse gods was doomed to a dark and gloomy life. His wisdom and ability to see into the future, when the gods would fall, lay heavy upon him. He is often pictured with two ravens,

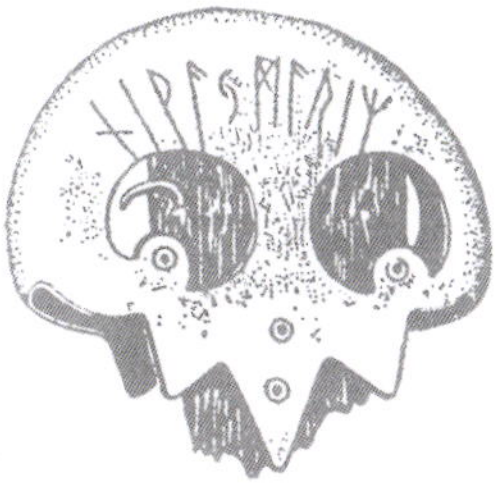

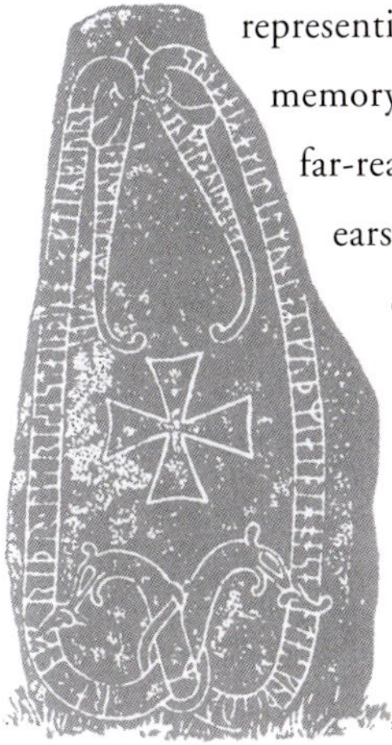

representing meaning and memory. They were his far-reaching eyes and ears, as they soared above the earth, constantly adding to his great wisdom. One of the many mystical achievements Odin is credited with is the formulation of the runes, symbols carved into stone. Aware that knowledge is only attained through sacrifice, he hanged himself from the branches of Yggdrasil, the tree of knowledge, for nine days and nights. This image is echoed on the Hanged Man card in the Tarot. Odin's body was not equal to the suffering and he died. But through his indomitable will he was reborn, bringing with him the knowledge of the world beyond. And from this came forth the runes.

Other Norse gods are related to the meanings of particular runes. Odin's son, Thor, is associated with thunder, fertility and the law. His hammer, a potent symbol equivalent to the Christian cross, was used to defeat the giants who forever threatened Valhalla. Frigga, Odin's daughter and wife, is the goddess of fertility. Loki, the wizard of lies, affects runes of knowledge and information, such as Rad and Ansur, by confusing and obfuscating. The interpretation of the runes was the prerogative of the shaman, a mixture of priest and magician.

Belief in the runes lasted well after Christianity had spread into northern Europe and outlived the Catholic church's ban of their use in 1639. Their use as an alphabet did not die out until well into the 19th century. Though some elements of the runic alphabet have been assimilated into Scandinavian languages, from that time they have been used exclusively as to divination.

The concentrated power of the stones, born out of the epic tales of the gods and the hardships of nature in cold and dark northern Europe, can now shine and illuminate. When the stones are swirled and turned, we have, literally, the distillation of a powerful oral tradition at our fingertips.

# THE RUNES

'Rune' means both 'secret' and 'whisper', reflecting the fact that their meaning has been passed down orally, like the epic poems of Iceland and the Celtic race. Those poems were eventually committed to manuscript, but there is no written runic literature.

There are several runic alphabets, deriving from different cultures. The most commonly consulted is the Elder Futhark or Older Alphabet. The word 'futhark' derives from the initial letters of the first six runes, Feoh, Ur, Thorn, Ansur, Rad and Kenn.

There are twenty-four runes, divided into three aetts or eights, each with traditional attributes and a composite meaning. To these has been added a blank rune, Wyrd, but it need not always be employed. The Younger Futhark, traced back only to around 700 ad, has only sixteen runes, whilst the Anglo-Saxon Futhark has varied between twenty-eight and thirty-three runes. Some of these runes simply have different spellings. For example Feoh becomes Fehu and Lagu becomes Laguz. Others have completely different names, such as Beorc, which becomes Berkana, the name of a tribe of fearsome warriors, from whom the word 'beserk' derives. But, whatever the name, the attributes remain largely the same.

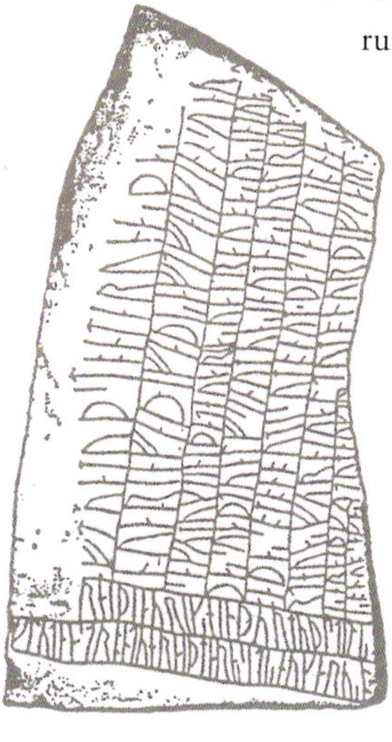

# FREY'S EIGHT

The Elder Futhark is made up of three groups of eight runes. The first group is named after Frey, god of fertility.

## FEHU

*Cattle, nourishment*

In many primitive cultures cattle represented wealth and prosperity and were a form of currency. As cattle needed hard work and careful nurturing, Feoh indicates earned wealth, rather than unexpected windfalls. Today, Feoh counsels caution and prudence and advises that in business matters a straight road should be followed. No changing of horses in mid-stream.

When reversed (upside down), Feoh indicates difficulties in financial matters, but, allied to more positive runes, these may be only temporary.

# UR

*Aurochs, promotion*

The aurochs was a wild bison, now extinct, which was something like the North American buffalo. In Germanic tribes, killing an aurochs was part of the rite of passage from youth to man. So, Ur represents proving oneself, discovering inner qualities to see you through sudden changes, often of a positive nature, such as promotion to greater responsibilities. In business, Ur suggests better fortune, through persistent effort.

When reversed its message can be cautionary rather than adverse. What may seem like an opportunity to be grasped, should be allowed to pass this time. Allied to positive rune combinations the situation will generally be for the good.

# THORN

*A thorn, protection*

Thor, the Great Protector, whose hammer was worn as an amulet, is related to Thorn. Protect yourself, not simply from enemies, but from over-indulgence and excessive ambition. Thorn protects by warning of an impending wrong choice, especially in relationships, either in money matters or love. Thorn, as Thor's Roman equivalent, Jupiter, suggests taking professional advice, from lawyers or doctors.

Thorn reverses, but not in the usual way. When upside-down it looks left to right. This eases any negative effects, but still suggests that a wrong course of action is about to be taken. This can have a positive aspect if the warning is heeded.

# ANSUR

*A mouth, communication*

Ruled by Mercury, the Messenger of the Gods, Ansur is the rune of communication, particularly between teacher and pupil or master and apprentice. It opens your mind to new ideas if faced with a practical or verbal test. An interview may be imminent, with Ansur suggesting a successful outcome. Though Mercury also rules travel, Ansur does not suggest that the questioner will go on a journey. More likely, a visitor can be expected, perhaps to offer guidance.

Ansur reversed means that advice given is not sound and that the guide or advisor does not have the questioner's best interests at heart, perhaps through some conflict of interest. With other negative runes it can even suggest that the questioner, like Mercury, will never grow up and mature. The Peter Pan syndrome.

# RAD

*A cartwheel, travel*

This rune represents not just physical travel, but the receiving and sending of messages. If a journey is indicated, it will more likely be for pleasure, than for business, and will be trouble-free. Rad is a rune of immediate action, be it a considered business move or a holiday taken on impulse. If involving business, Rad, when allied to other positive runes, virtually guarantees success. As it is related to Mercury, along with Ansur, it suggests travel to acquire learning. Rad, reversed, simply negates its good side. Expect frustrated or frustrating travel or business plans. Things aren't going to work out. Stay at home.

## KEN

*A torch, recovery*

A positive rune, Ken aids recovery in all its aspects, from business difficulties to health problems. After recovery, Ken offers you protection through its association with the fire gods, Mars and the Sun. This link also gives Ken special powers to predict strong sexual relationships and activity. If accompanied by runes of communication, Ken provides the spark of creative inspiration.

## GEOFU

*A gift, generosity*

Generosity of spirit and action mark Geofu, signifying the coming together of like minds, in love or business. But it is more important in matters of the heart and can mean much more than a new liaison. Marriage is in the air. One small drawback; though Geofu cannot be reversed, it can appear as a gift from the runes to confirm a problem, and those drawn with it cancel out the good intentions.

# WYNN

*Joy, illumination*

Wynn presages coming good fortune: health, wealth and happiness. The joy it brings can come from many sources, from family, friends or through contentment at work. Creativity comes with the opening of the mind to new ideas, often when the work in hand is practical; jewel-making, handicrafts or gardening. Together with runes of communication, it means good news is on its way. Doom and gloom are presaged by a reversed Wynn. So powerful are its positive aspects that equally powerful negative aspects have to prevail. Unsettled family life, unsuccessful travel and aggravation at the workplace. Hope it appears with more fortunate runes.

# HAGALL'S EIGHT

Primitive Teutonic tribes symbolized the oft-times disruptive forces of Nature by the rune Hagall, meaning hail. Events beyond their control took on magic significance and came to represent the disruptive forces in their everyday lives.

## HAGALL

*Hail, disruption*

Nature rules Hagall, the rune which represents immutable forces in our lives which we have to accept. In a reading it can look negative, as it invariably heralds some sort of disruption. As it cannot be reversed, the runes drawn with it become doubly significant, providing an element of stability or indicating which corner of life may be disrupted.

## NIED

*Necessity, patience*

Nied counsels patience during the adversity it can bring. Delays and limitations in business and impending ill-health are two in the catalogue of gloom brought by Nied. But it also brings fortitude to overcome adversity, forcing a closer look at an impending problem. When reversed, it compounds the problems, if its implicit warning is ignored.

## IS

*Ice, preservation*

The main attributes of Is appear to be wholly negative, ranging from delays in work to frosty relationships. Forturnately, as it cannot be reversed, these may only be temporary hitches. The runes drawn with Is are important indications of which area of your life is going to be affected. Look out, particularly, for relationship runes and be warned.

# GER

*Harvest, justice*

Ger indicates that you will reap the rewards of your labours, but, as it cannot be reversed, it can have a negative tendency. You may be about to reap punishment for past misdeeds. Ger can also herald change, as it represents the seasonal cycle. A change of employment or partner may be in the air, but with a positive aspect. Through its ruler, Mercury, Ger indicates legal matters, especially the associated paperwork. As with the harvest, patience is required. Legal wheels grind slowly.

# EOH

*A yew tree, resurrection*

The pliability of the yew tree, used over the centuries to make longbows, together with its symbolism in churchyards, make it the rune of resurrection. No matter how bad things seem, pick yourself up, dust yourself down and start all over again. Through its lunar influences, Eoh gives the strength to see you through what may seem like a major setback. In the end, this may well prove to be to your advantage. Eoh also suggests that you always keep your eye on your target, with realistic aims and ambitions.

# PEORTH

*A dice cup, disclosure*

Peorth predicts that something will be revealed, be it a hidden secret or some long-lost possession. As it is believed to represent a dice cup, Peorth predicts profitable gambling in business or for pleasure. Taking a risk could prove worthwhile. Unexpected rewards can be indicated. An inheritance from a long-lost relative would combine both of Peorth's attributes. Make that crucial move.

When Peorth is reversed, the revelations are of an unpleasant nature, betrayal and disappointment being among them. It suggests that it is not a good time to take a gamble of any sort. Luck is not on your side.

# EOLH

*An elk, protection*

Eolh is sometimes equated with the goddess Freya's amber necklace of protection. When it appears in a runecast it suggests that the questioner is in a charmed period. It is also a warning of problems which may be on the horizon. Eolh's sign is in the shape of an elk's antlers, which are drawn as a hand warding off troubles. The protection afforded is both spiritual and physical.

Reversed, Eolh suggests vulnerability, and not only physically. Watch your back at work. If you doubt a friend, you may have good reason and things may not be looking too good on the home front.

# SIGEL

*The sun, achievement*

In myth, the sun is always glorious, but it has a dark side. Sigel can point to great victories, particularly in business, but can also suggest serious overwork. The energy is there to cope, but when channelled in only one direction, results in tension. Varying your outlets is advisable. A mainly positive force, Sigel can indicate self-centredness and a lack of care for others. An irreversible rune, secondary meanings depend on fellow runes. Allied with negative Nied, it suggests fateful events. Watch your health.

# TYR'S EIGHT

The last group of runes is named after the God of War, the oldest of the North German deities. Like Odin, he represents both enlightenment and valour.

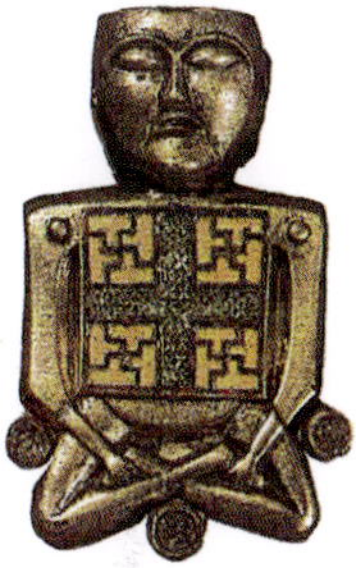

## TYR

*The god Tyr, motivation*

When Tyr appears in a reading a competitive, not combatative, character is suggested. High motivation is linked with great strength of will. Impressive stamina suggests that, when suffering difficulties, you will live to fight another day. It also represents fertility and increase, children and burgeoning ideas. When reversed, all the positive qualities are literally turned on their heads; impatience, lack of perseverence, low energy levels and a tendency to be accident prone.

# BEORC

*A birch tree, inception*

The birch tree was the tree of regeneration to the North European tribes. It represents the concept of mother and child, literally, and giving birth and nurturing a new idea, metaphorically. As one of its planetary rulers is Jupiter, a fortunate outcome is projected. Also ruled by the Moon, it can be read as a symbol of the mother and homemaker.

Reversed, it warns of family problems ranging from infertility to illness and death. Take heed, seek professional advice. If you do, these calamities can be averted.

# EHWAZ

*A horse, advancement*

This is the rune of controlled change, always for the better. The horse represents journeys and the trusting relationship between man and beast. The runes drawn with it will indicate the nature of the journey; a lengthy business transaction or long-term emotional involvement. When reversed, it does not automatically reverse its positive attributes. The meaning will depend on the runes drawn with it. If they are favourable, it remains favourable. If unfavourable, the attribute is reversed. Sometimes called Eh or Eoh, the Germanic name is used here to avoid confusion.

# MANN

*Mankind, interdependence*

As the ancient peoples depended upon each other to exist in difficult terrains, so this rune indicates that, if in difficulties, help is close by. This help will be objective advice or impartial action, perhaps by a professional advisor such as a doctor or lawyer. It indicates the gathering together of like-minded people to promote a good cause.

Reversed means that you are on your own, for the time being at least. Keep a low profile.

# LAGU

*Water, intuition*

The unpredictable waters of the northern seas were a constant danger to the Norsemen. In a reading, Lagu is a warning about the dangers during life's journey. Water's fluidity, controlled by the Moon, represents quicksilver thought, intuition and psychic powers. An artistic nature is indicated; design, painting, acting or writing.

When reversed, this is an unfavourable rune, needing the strongest favourable runes to temper its nature. Water spreads quickly, so take immediate action to contain the problem at hand.

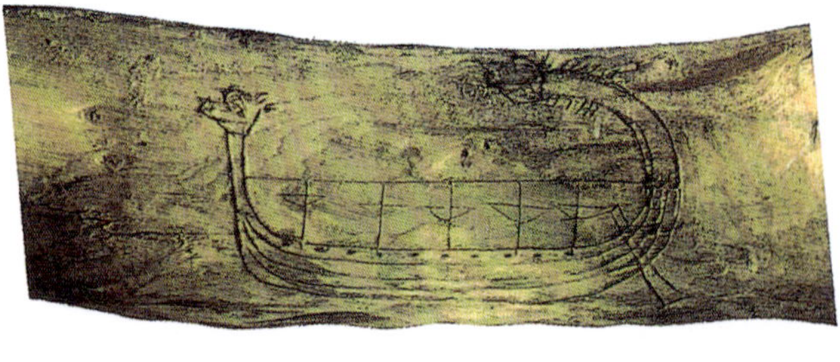

# ING

*Completion, new beginnings*

A weight off your mind, following the completion of a venture, is shown by this non-reversible rune, Your mind will be free, a clean sheet on which to inscribe a new idea. It can mean a feeling of completion by the forming of a perfect partnership in business or romance; two matched souls meeting. In general, its omens are good, but, occasionally, completion can bring endings in a negative sense, leaving a feeling of emptiness. Where do you go next?

# DAEG

*Day, transformation*

Daytime was of prime importance to the dwellers of the dark north, where night was often longer than day. The brilliance of the sun represents the life-force; growth and change, often of personality. The force of the sun suggests that the growth and change will be positive and successful. This is a non-reversible rune, with generally good signs. Its only negative aspect is that, as centre of the universe, it can indicate a tendency to self-centredness. Restrain yourself!

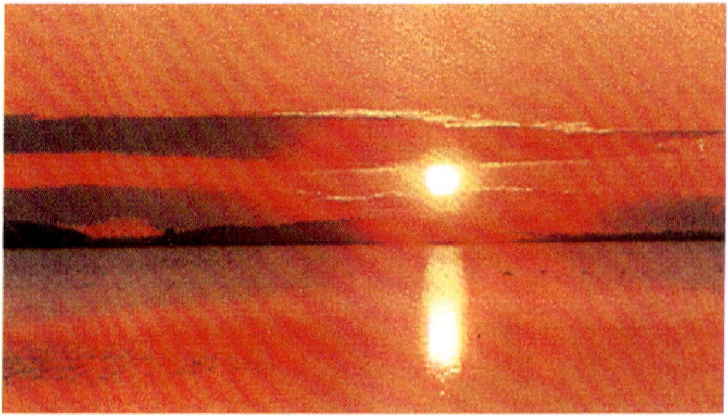

# OTHEL

*Possessions, inheritance*

As Feoh, the first rune, indicates earned wealth, so Othel represents accumulated wealth over the generations. This may mean accumulated knowledge, acquired attitudes or personal traits. Mundanely, it can refer to the family home, savings for your future or an unexpected inheritance. The dark side of the latter meaning is that, ultimately, to inherit there has to be a death. Othel reversed means giving something up, part of your inheritance, cultural or financial. You can become possessed by your possesssions. Learn the true value of things.

# MAKE YOUR OWN RUNES

Traditionally, rune signs are carved into stones, but they need not be. Your understanding and reading of the signs can be enhanced by making a personalized set of runes. You can even make several sets to use for different readings, but for basic readings it is best to establish a close relationship with one set. If you have a strong affinity with a gemstone, which need not be expensive, you can have a set engraved. Alternatively, you can use paint for the signs.

For those who love the sea, the runic alphabet can be painted on shells, but these will need careful handling because of their fragility. Smooth stones from the sea shore, collected at a favourite place, can also be used.

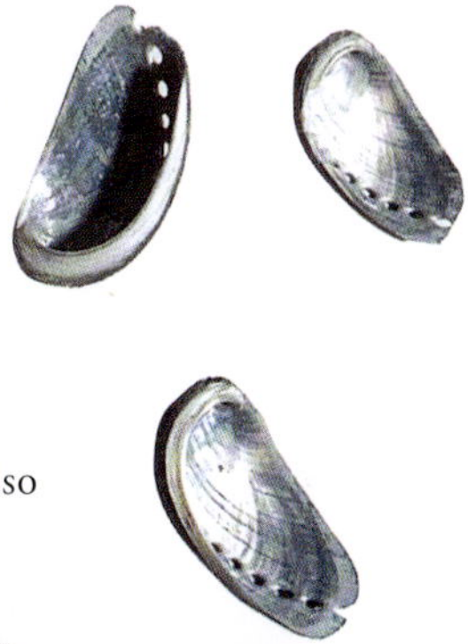

Wooden runes can be evocative of a glade or garden with special memories. They should not be made by taking cross-sections of branches, which are invariably round. This shape can cause confusion in determining whether or not a rune is reversed. Find a distinctive upright or oval shape.

# HOW TO CAST THE RUNES

Basic necessities for a casting are a set of runes in a bag and a neutral coloured cloth on which to lay them. But basics are not sufficient to draw forth the full power of the runes. They contain the accumulated knowledge of the ancients and should be treated as such. They are not a party game. There are excellent sets of runes available made of natural materials. Avoid synthetic or plastic ones if at all possible; they have no resonance with the ages.

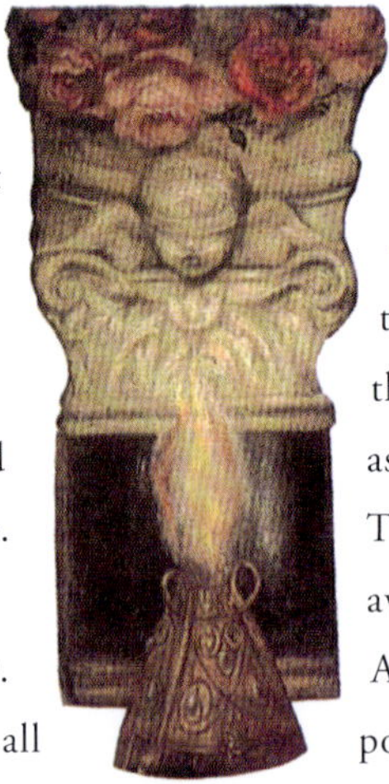

Before setting out to do a reading, create an atmosphere conducive to reception of messages. Do not make a great ritual, but arrange sensitive lighting, a candle or two, and burn a little incense or essential oil. One with a woodland fragrance might create an affinity with nature.

You may be casting the runes for your own benefit, or to answer questions and seek guidance for another. As with the Tarot and Chinese astrology, the emphasis is on guidance, rather than prediction.

You may select the number of runes required by picking them randomly from the bag and putting them in the pattern for the reading. More effective may be the method whereby all the runes are placed, face down, on the rune cloth. Swirl them around slowly and then pick those to which you feel particularly drawn. The physical contact may engender mental contact. But, beware! When using the latter method, it is possible that you may come to recognize the shapes of particular runes when face down.

# THE THREE NORNS

This is the simplest reading, named after Wyrd, the blank rune. It represents the Norns – the fates who constantly weave the threads of past, present and future. This rune is also known as 'the breastplate of the valkyries', the harbingers of fate.

Place all the runes, face down, on the cloth and swirl thoroughly. Turn them over and note which are upright and which reversed. With three positive runes the answer to the question asked is a resounding 'yes' and, when reversed, an equally resounding 'no'. If the question asked refers to the best time to sell some personal belongings, a reversed Feoh with two positive runes would suggest that the answer is 'yes' but the proceeds may not match expectations. Two positive runes, as pictured, might suggest a qualified 'yes', but the appearance of Wyrd negates this, suggesting that the Norns feel it would be better if the answer was not revealed now. Wyrd often appears when an ambiguous question is asked, such as 'Will I be happy if I move house?'. There can be many different answers, as happiness means different things to different people.

FEOH EOLH WYRD

# A SIMPLE CROSS READING

This is a good reading to use to familiarize yourself more with simple combinations of runes. It can be used for a blind reading; a reading for someone who has not asked a particular question. It is for you to ascertain the problem from the runes selected by the questioner, in this example a middle-aged woman.

In the cross, the central rune should give an indication of the question. Geofu suggests a query about the state of marriage, but not a problematic marriage. In fact, a seemingly happy one. Wynn in the 'past' position, confirms the view that it is a happy union and has been for some time. The future, indicated by Is, suggests that this is going to remain the situation. The 'help' rune, Eolh, adds yet further protection. Storm clouds appear with Hagell as a hindrance. But with such generally favourable omens, this is a small matter. If there is a problem it is simply that the woman in question can't believe her happiness and keeps having nagging doubts at the back of her mind. Can it last? The runes suggest it will.

# THE CELTIC CROSS

The Celtic Cross reading is adapted from the Tarot. It is useful for most questions; its only limitation is that it is best for guiding someone else, rather than yourself.

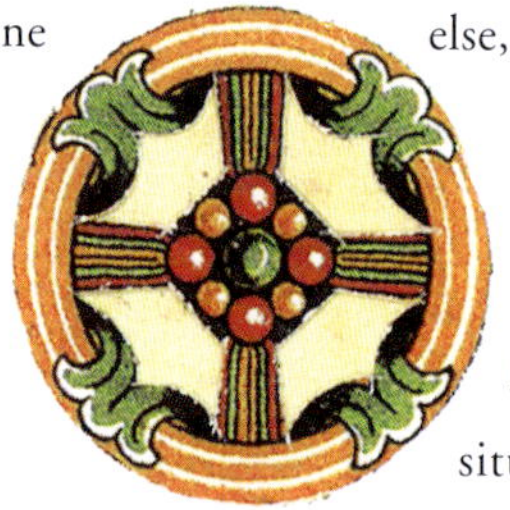

A young man asks how he can break out of a cycle of misfortune at home and work.

The present situation is confirmed by Feoh reversed, perhaps a loss of possessions. His problem is aggravated by Beorc reversed, revealing family troubles. Hagall suggests he should identify the outside influences affecting him, but Ansur assures that he will learn from these troubles. Rad indicates a move, physically or in his mind, which will be made possible by the pliability of Eoh. Eolh offers protection during his troubled progress, Ur suggests he has the inner strength to succeed. Geofu makes a timely appearance, a true ray of hope, tempering the lack of success which Nied presages.

The problems will stay for the time being. Perhaps he should heed Rad and get away for a time of reflection.

# RUNESCRIPTS

A runescript is a sequence of runes, rarely more than seven, selected personally and inscribed on a surface of your choice. This can be wood, fabric, a special paper or a pressed leaf. The purpose, while the runescript is on your person or somewhere nearby, is to create an aura of confidence if difficult decisions are in the offing, or if you have a wish you particularly want to come true. But runescripts are not magic. All they can do is help clear your mind as you contemplate them. If you are hoping to make money, a simple runescript, shown below, might help. Daeg stands

for growth and Feoh for earned wealth. The third rune is crucial. Here it is Is, the rune which 'freezes'. Your gains should be permanent.

In relationships, runescripts can ease matters. Analyse the problem and choose runes to alleviate it. Ken, the rune of new starts, is a good choice when allied to Geofu, the rune of partnership. The next rune, here, Feoh, suggests the problems may be financial, so should be balanced by Daeg, the rune of positive outcomes. Replacing Daeg with Is could make it permanent, but Wynn may be better as it strengthens a successful solution.

# RUNIC RELATIONSHIPS

Single runes, chosen at random, can provoke an instinctive reaction when contemplating a relationship, but, ultimately, it will always be a combination of runes which will give the best guidance. The positive power of the runes can counsel caution as well as passion.

Feoh suggests that affections will be returned, even a romantic conquest. Ur, a male rune, represents passion on the man's side of a relationship. Thorn advises that caution should be taken; play a waiting game. Ansur suggests that advice from a more experienced person would be helpful. Rad can bring companionship rather than undying love but warns of false friends. Ken confirms warm friendship, which may ignite into a more passionate

relationship. Geofu promises a union at hand, a gift from the gods, an equal partnership. Wynn is the object of your affection and the joy of that union. Hagall is the rune of disruption, but out of upsets good can come. A messy divorce may lead to a happy second marriage. Nydd means 'stick things out', you need a relationship, even if it may be

a sticky one. Is, generally, is not a good sign and can mean a cooling off in relationships, to the point of separation. Ger can indicate marriage, as it is the rune of legal contracts. Eoh warns not to overstate your case in love; take a restrained line. Peorth, the rune of gambling and secrecy, indicates sexual compatability. Eolh both protects existing relations and promises fruitful new ones. Sigel, the Sun rune, warns that self-centredness could adversely influence a relationship. Tyr, for women, represents the male partner, his strengths and weaknesses. Beorc is the rune of fertility, suggesting that a relationship is going to bloom. Ehwaz sees you between relationships, a period of change when help may be needed.

Mann exhorts you to understand yourself before you can understand others and, therefore, form a good relationship. Lagu's meaning can range from sexual passion to a long-lasting relationship. You will live happily ever after. Ing is another rune of fertility; perhaps a new love affair, a new family, is on the horizon. Daeg means transformation, a change of relationships or a changing relationship. Othel can mean the end of a relationship. It is the rune of death, not just physical, but mental and emotional.

# GARDENING RUNES

Runes have long been closely related to herbs, flowers and, indeed, all that grows. When gardening, green fingers can be made greener if they have recently held the rune relating to the particular plants you are tending. Simply keep it in your pocket whilst gardening.

In your flower garden you will find that Feoh encourages the lily of the valley, a hardy plant which multiplies profusely, while the assertively scented nasturtium belongs to Ur. Honesty, the plant, is related to Thorn, a rune concerned

with honesty, the moral concept. Ansur, rune of communication, represents the trumpet-shaped morning glory, while the bag shaped snap-dragon is aptly ascribed to Rad, a travel rune. Gorse is helped by Ken and its firebrand symbol and the rare lad's love is the flower of Geofu, another travel rune. Love-in-a-mist may be indicated by Wynn, the rune of joy and happiness, helpful if you are in a difficult partnership.

Hagall rules ferns and Nied looks after the crocus. Is is associated with the sweet pea, a plant symbolising relationships. Ger, rune of harvest, takes the cornflower, and Eoh, lilac. Meaning 'sedge', Eolh

looks after rushes, whilst Sigel, a healing rune, is connected with St. John's wort. Tyr symbolizes the red hot poker, as befits the God of War. Beorc takes the moonflower of birth and renewal. Mann copes with the poisonous foxglove, making it medicinally useful. Change is the attribute of Ehwaz's forsythia. Lagu's water lily is used as a cure, as is Ing's gentian. Marigold, related to Daeg, also has healing properties and we end on a note of hope with Odel ruling the snowdrop. If these attributes seem too specific, there are several ways in which they can be generalized. There are some 'umbrella' runes such as Hagall, which offers protection to plants being grown away from their natural habitats, tropical plants in a northern climate or delicate species requiring special surroundings, such as orchids. Similarly, Feoh could embrace a whole family of shrubs and Eolh, every sedge and fern.

# GEMS AND THE RUNES

Precious stones have had a place in occult mysteries since the earliest times and the Teutonic tribes were no exception. Malachite and lapis lazuli were sacred to the ancient Egyptians and the Chinese used jade for mystical effect.

Feoh is related to moss agate, each different-coloured variety having special properties. Ur belongs to the carbuncle, which brings high energy, and Thorn's sapphire offers protection. Ansur, the rune of communication, is oddly assigned the emerald, which signifies hidden knowledge. Rad's stone, chrysoprase is a form of mystic chalcedony, whilst bloodstone, assigned to Ken, is said to stop bleeding. Generally unlucky, the opal, given to Geofu, can be a helpful amulet; generally lucky, Wynn's diamond does nothing but bring good fortune. Hagall rules onyx, offering supportive strength and lapis lazuli, assigned to Nydd, can offer similar support in difficulties. The cat's eye, Is's stone, can see you through the night, just as Ger's cornelian offers help in dark hours.

Eoh's stone, the topaz, also induces contented sleep. Cool, clear aquamarine, ruled by Peorth, induces calmness, as does Eolh's gem, the amethyst. Fiery rubies help Sigel offer protection, Beorc's moonstone encourages relationships. Mann's blood-red garnet was thought to ward off plagues. Alone amongst the runes, Ehwaz rules two stones; Iceland spar when upright, offering direction and, when reversed, malachite, offering new

knowledge. The pearl of purity is given to Lagu, with warming amber being given to Ing. Daeg mainly rules the cheaper form of diamond, chrysolite, but surrounded by other favourable runes can assume the powers of diamond itself. Othel, rune of inheritance, rules the ruby, the rich, red gem of Mars.

The Wyrd, or blank rune, is not allocated a gem, but can be associated with the unlucky opal. The Norns were the Fates, opal is a fateful gem. Perhaps destiny intended them for each other. Wearing them may tempt fate or change your fate.

# ACKNOWLEDGMENTS

Illustrations are from the Folk Museum, Stockholm, the Civic Museum, Holstebro, Jutland, the Danish National Museum, Copenhagen, the Dusseldorf Kunstmuseum, the Niederosterreichesches Landsmuseum, Vienna, the Corcoran Collection and Grapharchive.

The publishers have made every effort to identify all illustration sources. any errors or omissions will be corrected in future editions.